Discover It Yourself

Solids and Liquids

KINGFISHER
LONDON & NEW YORK

KINGFISHER
LONDON & NEW YORK

Published 2021 by Kingfisher
Published in the United States by
Kingfisher, 120 Broadway,
New York, NY 10271
Kingfisher is an imprint of
Macmillan Children's Books,
London

Copyright © Macmillan Publishers
International Ltd 1993, 2021

Designed by: Tall Tree
Illustrated by: Diego Vaisberg/
Advocate Art

ISBN 978-0-7534-7674-1 (HB)
978-0-7534-7673-4 (PB)

First published in 1993 by
Kingfisher
This fully revised and updated
edition published
2021 by Kingfisher

Library of Congress Cataloguing-
in-Publication data has been
applied for.

Kingfisher books are available for
special promotions and
premiums. For details contact:
Special Markets Department,
Macmillan, 120 Broadway, New
York, NY 1027

Printed in China
9 8 7 6 5 4 3 2 1
1TR/0121/WKT/UG/128MA

Contents

Make sure you
have a grown-up
to help whenever
you see this sign.

!

What's It Made From?

Have you ever wondered what makes one thing different from another? A ball, a drop of water, and the wind are all very different because they are made from different materials. Most materials are solid, such as metal and wood. Solids don't change shape unless you cut, bend, or break them. Some solids, like glass, break easily. Some, like stone and many plastics, are very strong. Other materials are liquid. Water is a liquid. It flows and doesn't have a shape of its own.

Solids don't last forever. Glass breaks easily. Cloth and paper rot. Stone wears away, and some metals rust.

Eye Spy

Make a collection of different solids and decide whether they are made of wood, metal, plastic, stone, rubber, glass, or something else.

Here are five solid materials that look and feel different.

A third kind of material is gas. Air is a gas. You can't see it, and it is so thin that you can pass your hand through it. Yet you can feel air when it blows over your face and hands.

1. Rubber is light and grips well. It is also springy and returns to its original shape after being stretched.

2. Metals are strong. They can be sharpened into blades for cutting.

3. Glass is transparent (you can see through it), but it breaks if you drop it.

4. Plastic is strong, light, and waterproof. It doesn't rot or rust, and it can be made into any shape.

5. Most clothes are woven from fibers (fine threads). Woven fibers are strong and flexible—they bend easily.

DISCOVER IT YOURSELF!

Look more closely at your collection of solids through a magnifying glass.

See how cloth is made up of tiny woven threads. Glass, metal, and many plastics look shiny and smooth. Some rocks are made up of differently colored shiny grains.

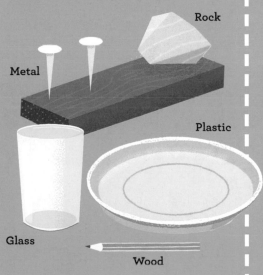

Metal

Rock

Plastic

Glass

Wood

Materials All Around

Everything we use is made from materials. Some, like cotton, come from plants. Others, like wool, come from animals. Many buildings are made from stone, which is cut or dug from the ground. Cotton, wool, and stone are all natural materials. Some natural materials can be made into other things. Oil can be made into plastics. Coal can be made into paint or soap. Coal and oil are called raw materials. Plastic is a manufactured, or artificial, material.

All plants and animals are made from many different materials. Two of the main ones are water and carbon. (Carbon is the black stuff in the middle of pencils.) In every human body there is enough water to fill four buckets and enough carbon to make over 1,000 pencils.

Wood into Coal

Oil is formed from the remains of ancient plants and animals. We drill for oil and dig for coal under Earth's surface, through layers of rock.

1. Millions of years ago, Earth was covered in thick forests and swamps.

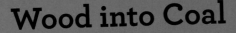

2. Fallen trees were gradually buried by thick layers of mud and sand.

3. The squashed wood slowly turned into coal.

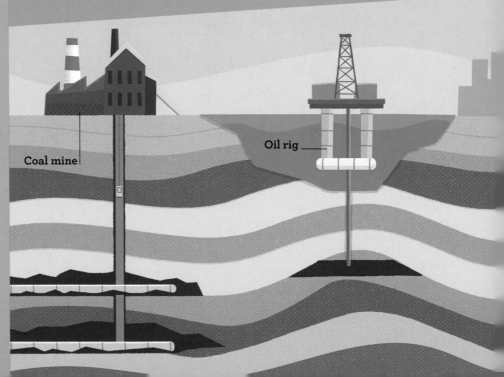

Coal mine

Oil rig

The air around us contains the gas oxygen. When we burn materials like coal and oil as fuels, they take oxygen from the air and give out heat (see next page). Food is a kind of fuel, too. All living things must have food and oxygen to power their bodies.

DISCOVER IT YOURSELF!

See how materials use oxygen when they burn. You'll need a small candle, a saucer, some water, and a glass jar.

1. Ask an adult to stick the candle to the bottom of the saucer with some melted candle wax, and then light the candle for you.

2. Pour about half an inch of water into the bottom of the saucer. Turn a glass jar upside down and carefully lower it over the candle. The glass should just sit in the water. Watch what happens to the flame.

Nitrogen (78%)
Oxygen (21%)
Carbon dioxide (0.03%)
Argon and other gases (0.97%)

Air is mostly made up of the two gases nitrogen and oxygen. It also contains water in the form of a gas (water vapor) and tiny bits of salt, dust, and dirt.

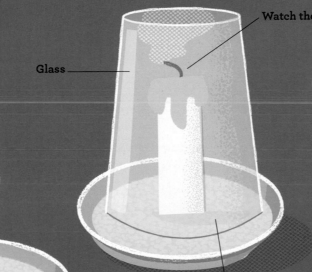

Watch the candle flame

Glass

Saucer or jar lid

Water level

? How It Works

The candle needs oxygen to burn. It therefore goes out when it has used up most of the oxygen in the glass. The water rises in the glass to take the space of the used oxygen.

7

Melting and Mixing

Have you ever sat in front of a roaring fireplace? The wood on the fire uses oxygen as it burns. The burning wood gives off heat and turns into ash. Heat changes materials. It can change solids into liquids, and liquids into gases. Heat can make things melt, make them cook, or set them on fire.

See how chocolate melts and becomes runny on a hot day—it changes from a solid to a liquid.

DISCOVER IT YOURSELF!

Find out how heat affects different materials. You will need three saucers, some ice, a bar of chocolate, some butter, and a wax candle.

Arrange a piece of each material around the edges of the saucers. (You'll need three pieces of each material.) Put one saucer in the refrigerator, one in a cool room, and one in sunlight or next to a hot fireplace.

• Which materials melt?
• Which go soft?
• Which stay solid?

	Chocolate	Ice	Butter	Wax
Hot spot				
Cool room				
Refrigerator				

✓✓ Melts
✓ Goes soft
● Stays solid

You could use a chart like this to record your results. Try testing some other materials in the same way.

8

DISCOVER IT YOURSELF!

See how some liquids will mix together while others don't mix at all, and how some solids dissolve (mix into a liquid).

Eye dropper

1. Mixing

Stir some milk into hot coffee to see how the milk and coffee mix to a beige color. Now try dropping a blob of ink or food coloring into some water to see how they mix together.

Food coloring

2. Unmixing

Pour equal amounts of vegetable oil and water into a clear plastic jar with a screw top. Screw on the top and shake the jar hard to try and mix the contents together. Leave the bottle to stand, and watch how the oil floats on top of the water in a layer.

Shake the mixture hard

3. Dissolving

When you stir sugar into a hot drink, it dissolves. Most things dissolve more easily in warm water than in cold. Try stirring the materials on the right into hot water and then cold water, and see what happens.

Instant coffee

Flour

Sugar

Salt

Sand

Powdered laundry detergent

Mixing Things Together

All solids, liquids, and gases are made up of chemicals. When some chemicals are mixed together, they react, or change, and new chemicals are made. Did you know that cooking is a kind of chemical reaction? When you bake a cake in the oven, all the things you put into the mixture react together to make a solid. Beating the cake mixture is important because it mixes in air—it's the air bubbles that make the cake light and fluffy.

Chemistry

Chemistry is the name for the part of science that is all about what things are made of and how they can be changed.

Eye Spy

Ask an adult to boil some red cabbage and then help you pour off some of the cabbage water into two dishes. Add lemon juice to one dish and baking powder to the second. Watch the chemical reactions make the water change color.

Red cabbage water on its own

With lemon juice

With baking powder

DISCOVER IT YOURSELF!

Make a chemical reaction that will power a rocket. You'll need a small plastic bottle with a screw top, a long piece of smooth string, a plastic straw, tape, tissue paper, vinegar, and baking powder.

1. Thread the string through the straw and stretch it out. Pour an inch and a half of vinegar into the bottle and tape the bottle to the straw.

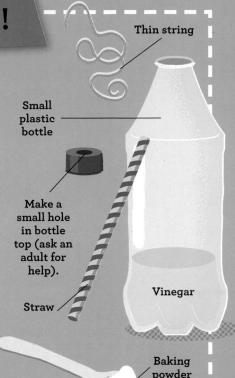

Thin string

Small plastic bottle

Make a small hole in bottle top (ask an adult for help).

Straw

Vinegar

Baking powder

Tissue paper

WARNING!

! You must do this experiment outside. It can be very messy!

2. Put a few teaspoons of baking powder into some tissue paper and wrap it into a bundle.

3. Gently slide the bundle into the bottle, trying to keep it out of the vinegar until you have screwed on the top of the bottle.

4. Give the bottle a shake, stand back, and wait for takeoff!

? How It Works

When baking powder and vinegar mix together, there is a chemical reaction and carbon dioxide gas is made. As more and more gas is made, the pressure builds up inside the bottle, shooting the gas out of the hole and pushing the bottle along the string.

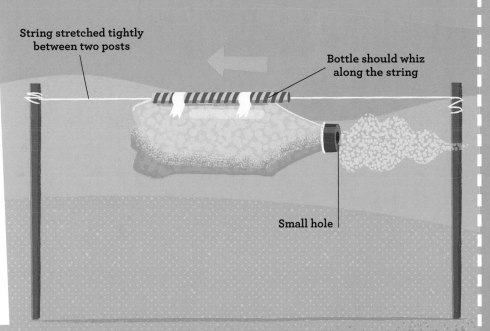

String stretched tightly between two posts

Bottle should whiz along the string

Small hole

Stone, Wood, and Clay

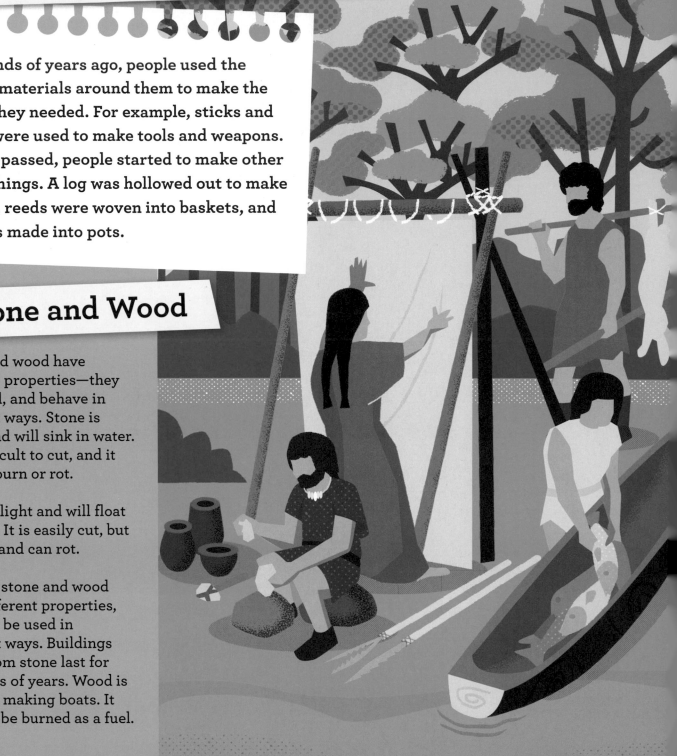

Thousands of years ago, people used the natural materials around them to make the things they needed. For example, sticks and stones were used to make tools and weapons. As time passed, people started to make other useful things. A log was hollowed out to make a canoe, reeds were woven into baskets, and clay was made into pots.

Stone and Wood

Stone and wood have different properties—they look, feel, and behave in different ways. Stone is heavy and will sink in water. It is difficult to cut, and it doesn't burn or rot.

Wood is light and will float in water. It is easily cut, but it burns and can rot.

Because stone and wood have different properties, they can be used in different ways. Buildings made from stone last for hundreds of years. Wood is good for making boats. It can also be burned as a fuel.

DISCOVER IT YOURSELF!

Try making thumb and coil pots from clay.
You could use them to keep things in.

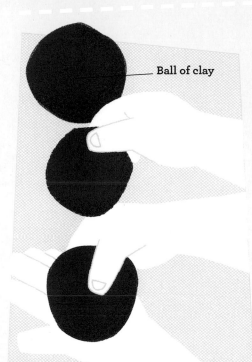

Ball of clay

Smooth the inside with water

Coil around to make sides

Roll out clay into thin sausages

Thumb Pots

Roll a piece of clay into a ball about the size of your fist. Stick your thumb into the middle of the ball to make a hole. Then turn the clay around your thumb while you shape the outside with your fingers.

Coil Pots

Roll out some long, thin clay sausages. Cut out a circle to make a base. Then coil the sausages around and around to make the sides.

If you can, bake your pots in a very hot oven called a kiln. Perhaps your school has one.

Firing a Pot

Before it is baked or "fired," a clay pot is very weak and crumbly—like a biscuit. Heat hardens the clay, making it much stronger and waterproof.

Ever since early times, potters have used a wheel to make pots. As the wheel turns, the potter shapes the clay with his hands.

Making Tools

Long ago, people chipped flints from huge stones and used them to make arrows, spearheads, and sharp blades for knives and axes. Their tools did similar jobs to tools we use today, but they were more clumsy and harder to handle.

Metal Tools

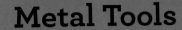

Most modern tools have sharp, light metal blades. Some have motors to make them work faster.

The Bronze Age

The Bronze Age started about 5,000 years ago. Bronze tools and ornaments have been found in the Middle East, China, and Europe.

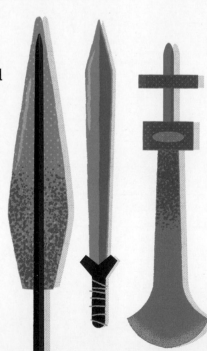

The Iron Age

About 3,000 years ago, people found a way to separate iron from rocks. Iron is harder than bronze. Tools made from iron are stronger and can be sharpened more easily.

14

Later, people began to make better tools from metals. They discovered a way of heating certain types of rocks so they could get copper out of them. Then they found that when they melted tin and copper together, it made a new material—bronze.

Copper and tin are fairly soft and flexible on their own, but bronze is hard enough to be used for sharp knife blades and ax heads.

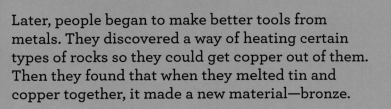

Bronze ax head

Copper

Tin

Bronze

Eye Spy

Visit a museum and look out for stone, bronze, and iron tools and weapons. You'll find that the wooden handles have rotted away.

Metal Magic

Strong Metal

We now use more than 50 kinds of metal, and most of them are found in rocks. Some of the more common ones are iron, copper, tin, aluminum, silver, gold, and chromium. Because each type of metal has different properties, they can be used in different ways. Some metals are better for making cars and others for making coins.

Steel is very strong. Steel wires and girders are often used to make bridges. Steel is mainly iron with a small amount of carbon mixed in it to make the iron stronger and harder.

Flexible Metal

Pure metals (metals that have not been mixed with anything else) are rather soft and flexible. They are used for wires or pipes.

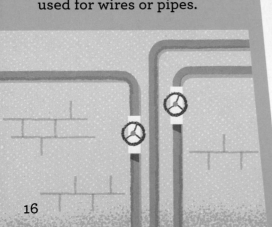

Heavy Metal

Almost all metals are heavier than water, so they sink. Lead and brass are two of the heaviest metals. They are often used to make weights.

Liquid Metal

All metals melt into thick liquids when they get very hot. Mercury is special. It is the only metal that stays liquid when it is cool.

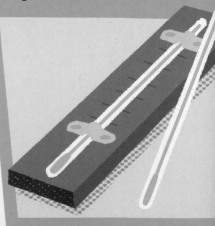

DISCOVER IT YOURSELF!

Use these four tests to help you decide whether something is made from metal.

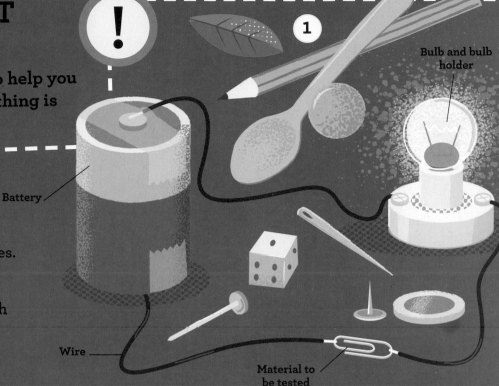

Battery

Bulb and bulb holder

Wire

Material to be tested

1. Does it carry electricity?

Test your material with a battery, a bulb, and two wires. All metal conducts, or carries, electricity. For the test to work, you must touch the wires on bare polished metal, not on paint.

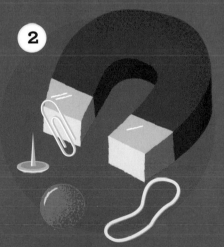

2. Is it magnetic?

If your material is attracted or "pulled" by a magnet, then it contains the metal iron. If not, then it may still be a metal like copper or aluminum (which aren't magnetic).

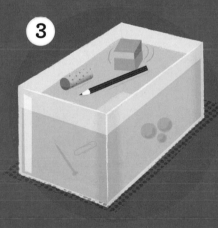

3. Does it float or sink?

All common metals are heavier than water, so they will sink. Therefore, if your material floats on water, it is not a metal and must be made of something else.

4. Can it be polished?

Most metals can be polished to a bright shine. Metals reflect light, so they can be used as mirrors. If you can see through your material, then it isn't a metal.

Useful Plastics

Plastics are not natural materials. They're made in factories from the chemicals found in oil. The chemicals are heated in steel tanks, which are kind of like huge pressure cookers. When the chemicals stick together, new plastic materials are made. Plastics are lighter and more flexible than metals, but they aren't as strong. Plastics can melt or burn when they are heated. An important property of plastic is that it doesn't conduct electricity, so plastic is wrapped around electric wire to make the wire safer.

Plastic gets soft when it's heated, so it can be made into all sorts of shapes, like these toys.

Plastic canoes and safety helmets don't crack or shatter when they get knocked.

Eye Spy

Put an empty yogurt cup in a bowl. Ask an adult to pour some very hot water over it. Watch how the plastic cup softens and changes shape.

Boiling water

Yogurt cup

DISCOVER IT YOURSELF!

Make some rubbery plastic at home from milk and vinegar.

1. Ask an adult to warm some creamy milk in a pan. When the milk is simmering, slowly stir in a few teaspoons of vinegar.

Creamy milk

Vinegar

2. Keep stirring, but just before the mixture becomes rubbery, add some food coloring.

3. Let the plastic cool and wash it under cold running water.

Stretchy, Strong, or Brittle?

Find some different kinds of plastic and try bending and stretching them. Are they stretchy and weak or stretchy and strong? Or are they brittle (do they snap easily)?

Plastic can holder

Plastic spoon

Plastic wrap

Homemade plastic

19

Springy Rubber

Rubber is made from a white juice, called latex, that comes from rubber trees. At factories, the liquid latex is made into solid rubber by adding an acid—just like you added vinegar (an acid) to the milk in the activity on page 19. Then the rubber is squeezed, dried, and shaped. Rubber is a useful material because it is so elastic. It can be stretched and squashed and it will still bounce back into shape.

Latex drips slowly into a collecting cup from grooves cut into the bark of a rubber tree. About one teacup of latex is collected each time.

Eye Spy

See how different types of materials slide less easily (make more friction) than others.

Eraser

Pencil

Wooden board

Coin

Washer

Rubber brake pad

1. Put an eraser on one end of a wooden ruler or board. Then gradually lift the end of the wood until the eraser starts to slip.

2. Try the same test with a metal coin or washer and a pencil. See how high you have to lift the wood before each material starts to slip.

? How It Works

The eraser will move last. This is because erasers are made from rubber, and rubber doesn't slide easily on smooth surfaces. That's why rubber is used for the brake pads on your bike. The rubber grips the metal wheel rim, and friction slows the wheel down.

DISCOVER IT YOURSELF!

Make your own rubber-powered machines.

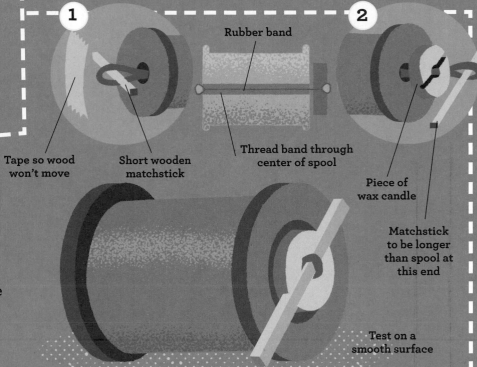

1 Tape so wood won't move · Short wooden matchstick

Rubber band · Thread band through center of spool

2 Piece of wax candle · Matchstick to be longer than spool at this end

Test on a smooth surface

Spool Tank

Thread a rubber band through the middle of an empty spool. Secure the band at both ends, as shown in drawings 1 and 2.

Wind up the band by turning the longer piece of wood until you cannot turn it anymore. Place it on a smooth surface, then let go!

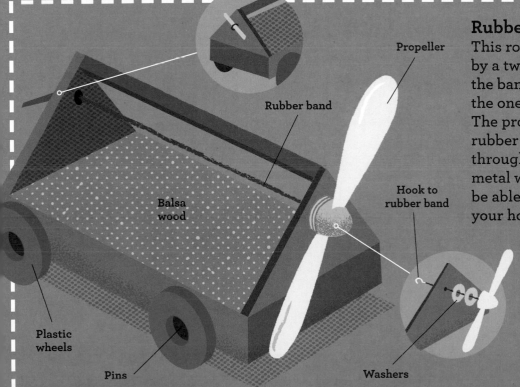

Rubber band · Balsa wood · Plastic wheels · Pins · Washers · Propeller · Hook to rubber band

Rubber Roadster

This roadster is also powered by a twisted rubber band. Here, the band turns a propeller—like the ones found in modeling kits. The propeller is attached to the rubber band with a hook that runs through the balsa wood and two metal washers. (You might be able to find the washers around your home, or you can buy them inexpensively from a hardware store.)

Why not hold a competition to design the fastest rubber-powered vehicle?

Flexible Fibers

Fibers are simply long, thin flexible strands or threads. We use both natural fibers, from plants and animals, and artificial fibers, from oil and coal. Cotton comes from the seed pods of the cotton plant, and wool comes from sheep. String can be made from plant fibers, and nylon is made from the chemicals in oil. Plant, animal, and artificial fibers can all be woven to make different kinds of cloth. Look at the labels in your clothes. Some will be made from mixtures of fibers, like cotton and nylon, or cotton and polyester.

A hair is a fiber. Animal fur is just a thick coat of hair. It traps tiny pockets of air between the fibers, keeping in the warmth.

Eye Spy

Collect some different fibers and look at them through a magnifying glass. Are they smooth or rough, thick or thin? Wool and twine are much rougher than nylon.

Nylon   Twine   Wool yarn   Cotton thread

Paper is made of fibers, too. Usually it's made of wood fibers. The wood is separated into fibers by crushing it to a pulp in water. The pulp is then squeezed into thin sheets and dried.

If you look at a piece of cloth and a piece of tissue paper under a magnifying glass, you can see the fibers clearly. The fibers in cloth are woven together evenly. But the fibers in paper are just squashed together in a jumble.

Making It Waterproof

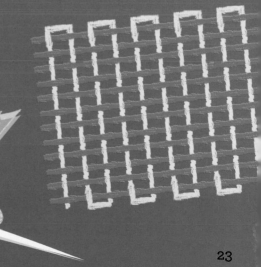

Secure with rubber band

Cloth is not usually waterproof because of all the tiny holes between the fibers. Try making a piece of cloth waterproof by rubbing it with some candle wax to gum up the holes. See if it has worked by wrapping the cloth around the top of a container filled with water and then tipping the container upside down.

DISCOVER IT YOURSELF!

Try weaving a piece of cloth with some wool.

1. Cut a row of triangular grooves in opposite sides of a piece of cardboard.

2. Wind a strand of yarn around the card as shown. This is called the warp.

3. Thread the needle with another strand of yarn and weave it in and out of the warp thread. This is the weft.

4. When you've finished, knot the end and cut the warp threads so that you can remove the cardboard.

Stiff cardboard

Warp

Weft

23

Strong but Brittle

Glass is made from sand—just like the sand on a beach. The sand is heated with limestone and other materials until they melt and mix together. The red-hot mixture is poured into different shapes. It then cools and sets to solid glass. Glass is a very useful material. Because it's transparent, we use it for windows and lenses. It's also waterproof and easy to clean, so it is used to make bottles and jars.

Although glass is strong and hard, it is also brittle. This means that it can shatter easily. A glass bottle can carry a heavy weight without breaking, but a sudden knock can make it shatter. Have you ever dropped a glass and seen it break into sharp pieces? (Don't test this out, though, you could hurt yourself!)

When broken glass is especially dangerous, a special safety glass is used (see next page).

Some glass bowls or ornaments are made by glass blowers. They pick up a blob of soft glass on the end of a hollow tube. Then they blow into the tube and the glass blows up like a balloon.

24

Making It Strong

A tennis racket must be strong enough to hit a ball without breaking. A bridge needs to be able to take the weight of all the traffic that uses it. Things must be made so that they are safe and strong enough to last. To make something strong, you must use a strong material and make it into a strong shape.

Wonderful Webs

The silken strands in a spiderweb are thinner than the hairs on your head, but they are stronger than steel of the same thickness!

Safety Glass

Car windshields are usually made of safety glass. The glass may still shatter, but the pieces won't fly into the driver's face because they're held in place by a sheet of clear plastic sandwiched between two glass sheets.

Concrete Strength

Many buildings are made out of concrete, which is a mixture of cement, water, and gravel or sand. Because concrete can crack if it is stretched, it is often reinforced (made stronger) by thin steel rods set into the mixture.

Carbon Fibers

Fibers made from carbon are flexible, light, and strong. They are used to make parts of bikes, tennis rackets, and aircraft bodies. Carbon fibers weigh about a fourth as much as steel, but they are twice as strong.

DISCOVER IT YOURSELF!

See if you can design a strong bridge shape.

Sydney Harbour Bridge in Australia is made of steel. It carries eight lanes of traffic and two railroad tracks.

1. First try experimenting with paper bridge shapes. Paper is much too flexible to make a flat bridge, but if you fold the paper, the bridge can be made much stiffer and stronger. Three strong bridge shapes are shown below.

2. Try making a bridge frame out of straws. Join the straws by pushing the end of one into the end of another then adding sticky tape. You could test your bridge's strength by seeing whether it can take the weight of a yogurt cup filled with sand.

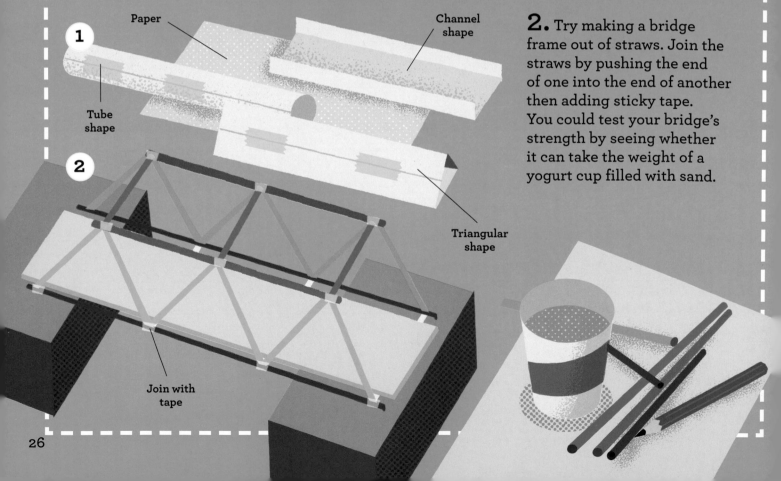

1

Paper

Channel shape

Tube shape

2

Triangular shape

Join with tape

Rusting and Rotting

Almost all materials wear out. Most do not last forever. Have you ever left your bike in the rain? Did it rust? Iron rusts when it gets damp—it reacts with water and oxygen in the air, and eventually pieces of the metal crumble to a brown powder. Wood rots if it gets too damp. Fungus grows on it, and the wood loses its strength. Even stone can wear away. It can crack and crumble in frost and rain.

Some types of rock are softer than others. Here, the continuous pounding of waves has gradually worn away the cliffs.

Eye Spy

Look out for insect holes in old furniture and trees. Some insects eat wood—termites and woodworms can destroy whole buildings. There is even a bee that makes holes in brick walls. The masonry bee burrows into the mortar between bricks to lay its eggs.

Gold is the only metal that doesn't rust, even when it is buried in the ground for thousands of years. Because it stays so bright, gold is called the "noble metal."

DISCOVER IT YOURSELF!

Find out what makes iron rust. You'll need four iron nails, four glass jars (one with a lid), and some clear nail polish.

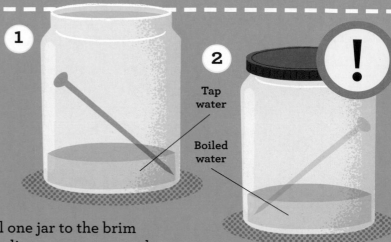

Screw top

Tap water

Boiled water

1. Fill one jar to the brim with ordinary tap water and drop a nail into it.

2. Ask an adult to boil some water for you. Leave the water to cool until it is lukewarm. Pour the water into another jar, making sure that it is full to the brim. Drop the second nail into the jar and screw on the lid. (Ordinary water has air in it. Boiling the water gets rid of the air, and putting a lid on the jar stops fresh air from getting into the jar.)

3. Paint the third nail all over with clear nail polish. Drop this nail into a jar of tap water. Don't put a lid on the jar.

4. Drop the fourth nail into an empty jar. Again, don't screw on a lid.

Look at the jars every day to see which nails are getting rusty and which aren't.

Painted nail

Clear nail polish

? How It Works

Iron only rusts when both air and water are present. So you will probably find that the nail in the tap water rusts most quickly. The third nail is protected by nail polish. The nail polish keeps the air and water away from the iron and stops it from rusting.

New from Old

This recycling plant sorts out different metals. The steel will be reused to make new containers.

Using It Again

Have you ever counted how many glass bottles, metal cans, or plastic containers are discarded in your house in a week, or a month? Instead of throwing away glass, metal, and plastic, you can help the environment by using them again. Recycling reduces the amount of trash we make and saves energy and money.

DISCOVER IT YOURSELF!

See which things rot away.

Dig a hole and bury a soda can, a glass jar, a plastic container, paper, and some apple. Mark the place with a stick. Dig it up after two weeks to see what's left.

Don't forget to take your trash away after two weeks.

? How It Works

Worms and other tiny creatures will have begun to eat the food and paper. These things are biodegradable. The glass, metal can, and plastic would just lie in the soil for years.

DISCOVER IT YOURSELF!

Recycle and reuse the things you use. Every little bit helps, so if you don't already recycle your trash, start now!

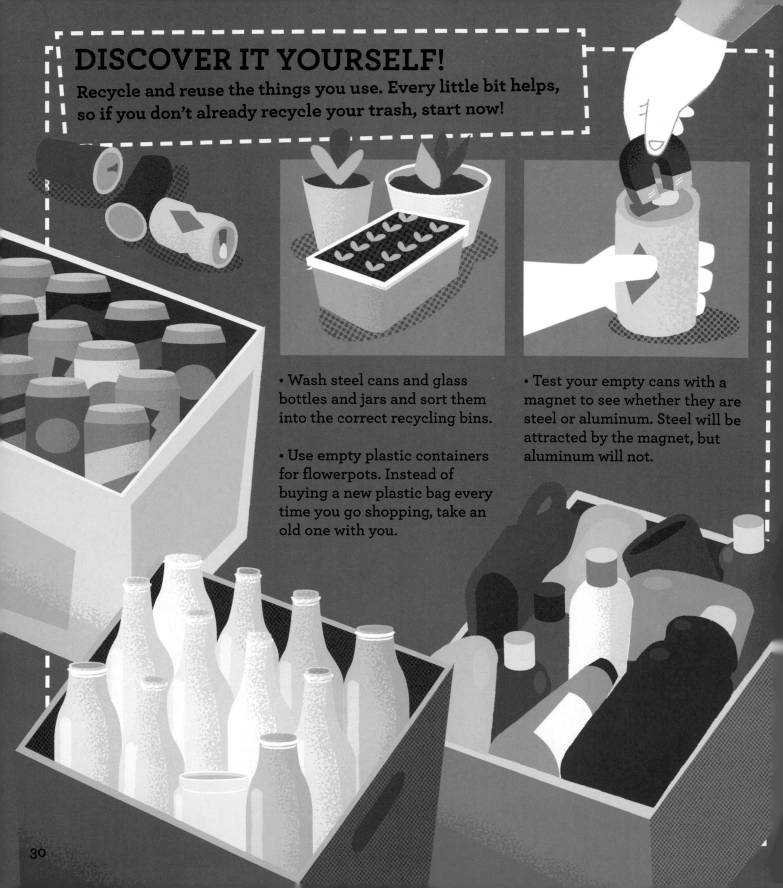

• Wash steel cans and glass bottles and jars and sort them into the correct recycling bins.

• Use empty plastic containers for flowerpots. Instead of buying a new plastic bag every time you go shopping, take an old one with you.

• Test your empty cans with a magnet to see whether they are steel or aluminum. Steel will be attracted by the magnet, but aluminum will not.

Using Trees

It takes around 3 gallons (11 L) of water to make one sheet of paper, and a whole tree to make 230 newspapers or magazines.

In Africa, a project called the Great Green Wall has a plan to build a wall of trees that stretches across the width of the continent—that's 5,000 miles (8,000 km) long!

• Open envelopes carefully so you can reuse them to send your letters, and buy sticky labels to place over the old address. You can even save the used stamps to give to stamp clubs.

• Buy recycled paper for painting and drawing.

• Save and bundle up old papers and comic books so that the paper can be recycled.

Save a Tree!

Every year, four billion trees are cut down around the world to make paper. That's like cutting down 1 percent of the Amazon rain forest—every single year. All around the world forests are shrinking. The rain forests are in most danger. Not enough new trees are planted to replace the ones that are being cut down.

Index